7 SUBJECT
SCIENCE
PORTFOLIO
MINECRAFT
& THE REAL WORLD

PHYSICS

GEOLOGY

CHEMISTRY

METEOROLOGY

BOTANY

ZOOLOGY

TECHNOLOGY

Study Seven Branches of Science!

7 SUBJECT SCIENCE PORTFOLIO MINECRAFT
& THE REAL WORLD

Fun-Schooling With Thinking Tree Books

By: Isaac J. Brown,
Sarah Janisse Brown
& Tolik Trishkin

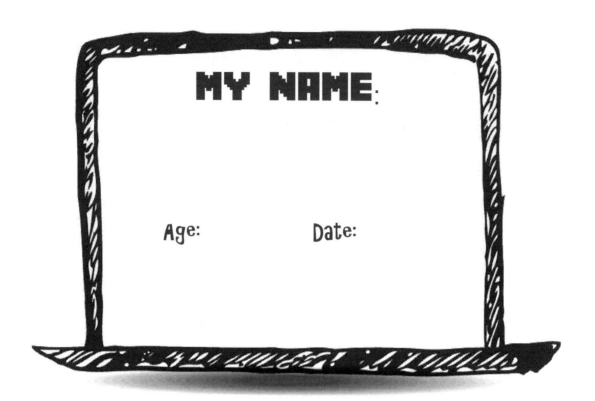

MY NAME:

Age: Date:

HOW TO USE THIS BOOK:

1. Choose four books and two documentaries about each scientific subject.

2. Ask your teacher how many pages to complete each day.

3. Be ready to build something in your Minecraft world based on each scientific subject.

4. Use gel pens and colored pencils to complete the activities that require color.

TABLE OF CONTENTS:

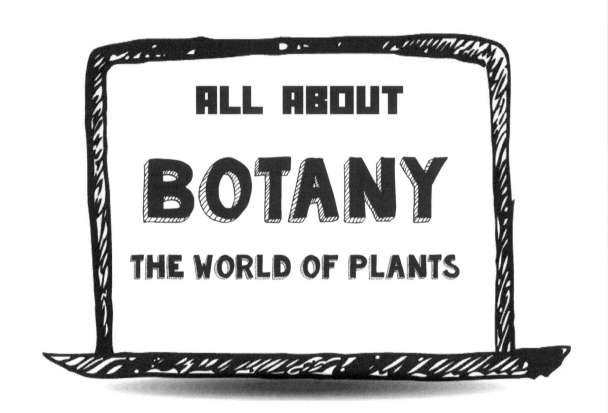

ALL ABOUT
BOTANY
THE WORLD OF PLANTS

WHAT IS

BOTANY?

Botany is the scientific study of plants.

"Plants," to most people, means a wide range of living organisms from the smallest algae to the largest living things – the giant Sequoia trees. Plants are living things which make their own food by using the energy from sunlight to combine carbon dioxide and water into sugars

By this definition plants include: algae, fungi, lichens, mosses, ferns, conifers and flowering plants.

MY BOOKS ABOUT
BOTANY

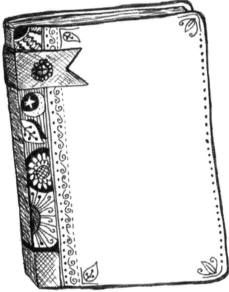
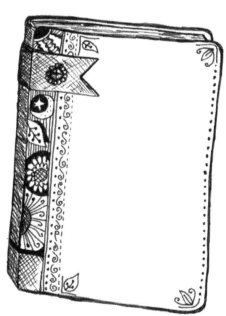

BOTANY

READING TIME

Today's Date:

_____

Write and draw about what you are reading.

Date:

READING TIME
Copy an interesting or important paragraph or list from your book.
Book Title:_____ Page #_____

_____
_____
_____
_____
_____
_____
_____
_____
_____
_____
_____
_____
_____
_____
_____
_____
_____

Illustration 1

Illustration 2

Botany - The World of Plants

Draw a plant cell here and design a plant cell in Minecraft.

My Notes

_____
_____
_____
_____
_____
_____
_____
_____

Botany – The World of Plants

Plant Cell

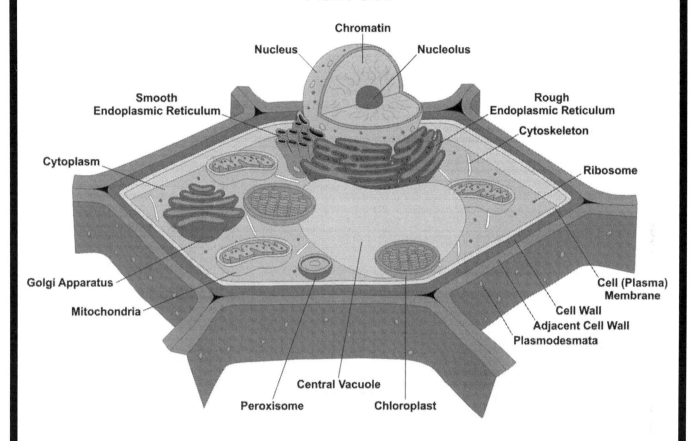

Chromatin

Nucleus

Nucleolus

Smooth Endoplasmic Reticulum

Rough Endoplasmic Reticulum

Cytoskeleton

Cytoplasm

Ribosome

Golgi Apparatus

Cell (Plasma) Membrane

Mitochondria

Cell Wall

Adjacent Cell Wall

Plasmodesmata

Central Vacuole

Peroxisome

Chloroplast

My Notes

Date:

WATCH A BOTANY
DOCUMENTARY

Title:_____

Draw a scene from the documentary:

Write a review:

_____
_____
_____
_____
_____

14

WHAT I LEARNED

Date:

Topic:_____

_____
_____
_____
_____
_____
_____
_____
_____
_____
_____
_____
_____
_____
_____
_____
_____

Draw a diagram or illustration:

Date:

_____

SCIENCE EXPERIMENTS
& OBSERVATIONS

Look online, or in your science books, for an interesting plant-related experiment that you can do at home. Explain and draw the process and your findings here.

CREATE A MINECRAFT & SCIENCE
COMIC STRIP

Date:

BOTANY
& THE
WORLD OF
PLANTS

VOCABULARY BUILDING

Look in your science books
for **FOUR** words with more than **TEN** letters.
Write the words and their definitions below:

MINECRAFT & THE REAL WORLD

What topic are you Learning About?

_____

Draw an example from Minecraft:

Draw an example from the real world:

MINECRAFT
DESIGN TIME

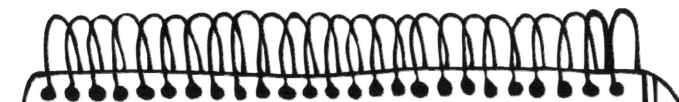

Botany - The World of Plants
Plant an oak tree in Minecraft.

Life Cycle of an Apple Tree:

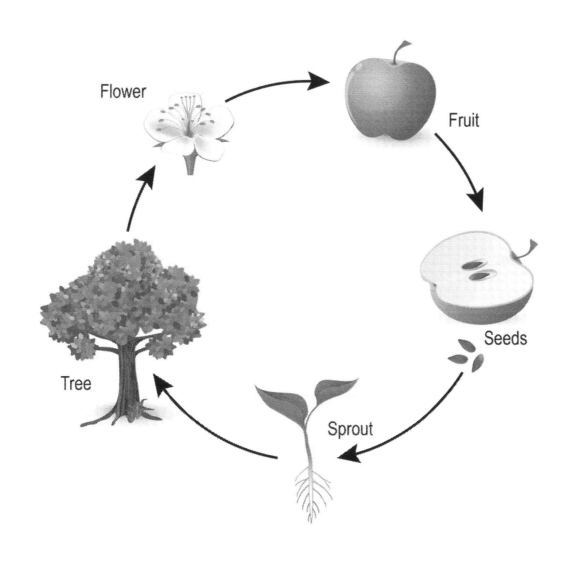

Flower

Fruit

Seeds

Tree

Sprout

SCIENCE AND GEOGRAPHY

RESEARCH THE SCIENTIFIC DISCOVERY OF YOUR CHOICE:

WHERE IN THE WORLD DID THE DISCOVERY TAKE PLACE?

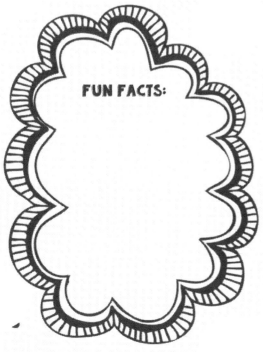

FUN FACTS:

DRAW THE DISCOVERY:

AMAZING SCIENTIFIC DISCOVERIES
CHOOSE A PERSON TO STUDY

Date:

Name: _____

BIOGRAPHY:

_____
_____
_____
_____
_____
_____
_____
_____
_____
_____
_____
_____
_____
_____
_____

Draw a diagram or illustration:

LISTENING TIME
Draw and doodle
while listening to an audio book.

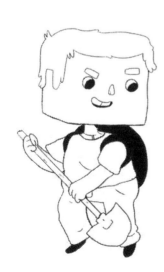

Today's Date:

_____

READING TIME

Write and draw about
what you are reading.

Date:

READING TIME
Copy an interesting or important paragraph or list from your book.
Book Title:_____ Page #_____

_____
_____
_____
_____
_____
_____
_____
_____
_____
_____
_____
_____
_____
_____
_____
_____

| Illustration 1 | Illustration 2 |

Botany - The World of Plants
Draw the anatomy of a leaf

My Notes

_____
_____
_____
_____
_____
_____
_____
_____

Botany - The World of Plants
Leaf Anatomy

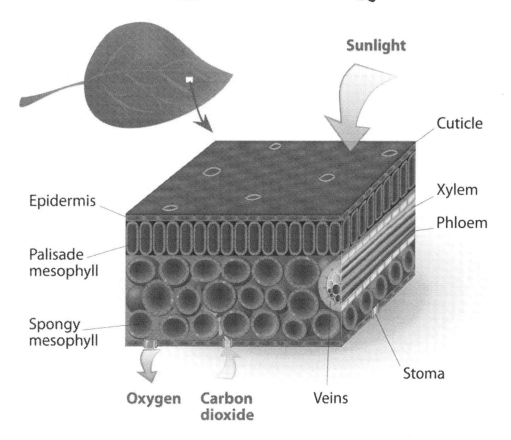

Sunlight

Cuticle

Xylem

Phloem

Epidermis

Palisade mesophyll

Spongy mesophyll

Stoma

Oxygen

Carbon dioxide

Veins

My Notes

Date:

WATCH A BOTANY DOCUMENTARY

Title:_____

Draw a scene from the documentary:

Write a review:

_____
_____
_____
_____
_____

BOTANY WHAT I LEARNED

Date:

Topic:_____

_____

_____

_____

_____

_____

_____

_____

_____

_____

_____

_____

_____

_____

_____

_____

_____

Draw a diagram or illustration:

Date:

_____

SCIENCE EXPERIMENTS & OBSERVATIONS

Look online, or in your science books, for an interesting plant-related experiment that you can do at home. Explain and draw the process and your findings here.

CREATE A **MINECRAFT** & SCIENCE
COMIC STRIP

Date:

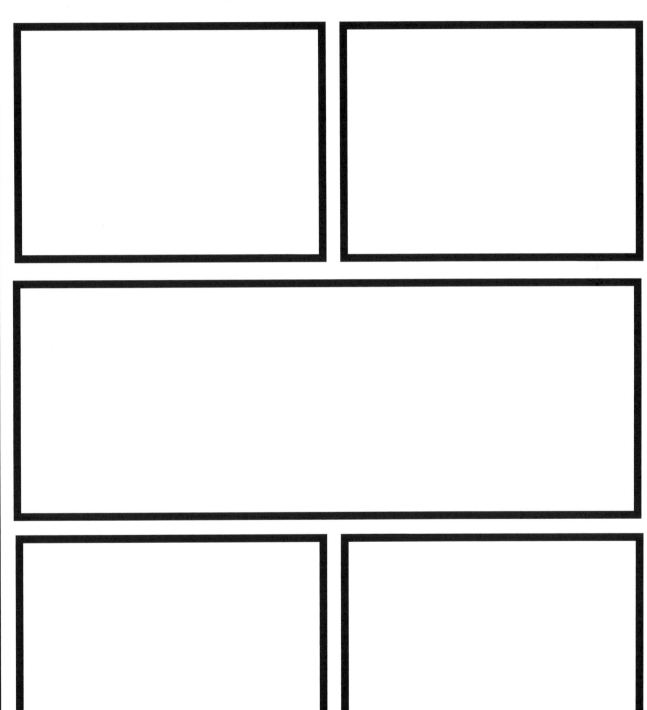

VOCABULARY BUILDING

Look in your science books
for **FOUR** words with more than **TEN** letters.
Write the words and their definitions below:

MINECRAFT & THE REAL WORLD

What topic are you Learning About?

_____

Draw an example from Minecraft:

Draw an example from the real world:

MINECRAFT
DESIGN TIME

BOTANY - THE WORLD OF PLANTS

Draw your favorite plant that
you can grow in Minecraft, and draw your favorite
plant from the real world.

Botany - The World of Plants
Nature Study

Draw a plant or tree that you
see outside today.

SCIENCE AND GEOGRAPHY

RESEARCH THE SCIENTIFIC DISCOVERY OF YOUR CHOICE:

WHERE IN THE WORLD DID THE DISCOVERY TAKE PLACE?

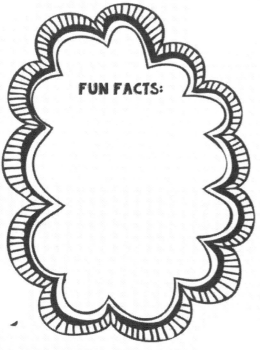

FUN FACTS:

DRAW THE DISCOVERY:

AMAZING SCIENTIFIC DISCOVERIES
CHOOSE A PERSON TO STUDY

Name: _____

BIOGRAPHY:

_____
_____
_____
_____
_____
_____
_____
_____
_____
_____
_____
_____
_____
_____
_____

Draw a diagram or illustration:

LISTENING TIME
Draw and doodle
while listening to an audio book.

Botany - The World of Plants
Design a farm or garden in Minecraft.

My Notes

_____
_____
_____
_____
_____
_____
_____
_____

Botany - The World of Plants

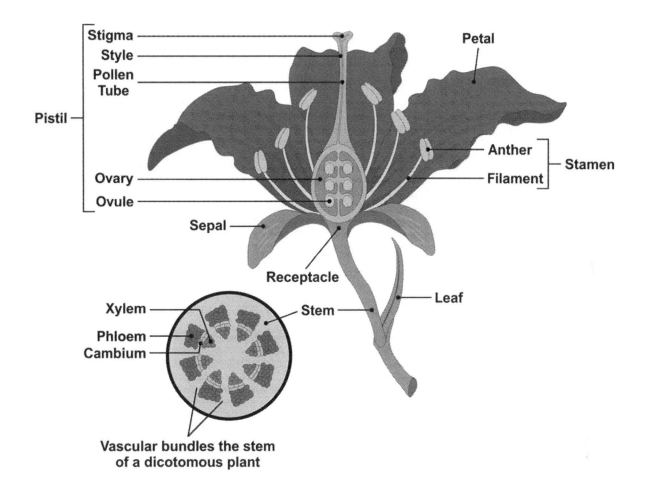

Stigma
Style
Pollen Tube
Pistil
Ovary
Ovule
Sepal
Receptacle

Petal
Anther
Filament
Stamen
Leaf
Stem

Xylem
Phloem
Cambium

Vascular bundles the stem of a dicotomous plant

My Notes

OCCUPATIONS

Would you like this job? YES - NO - MAYBE

BOTANY TECHNICIAN

What would the world be like if no one did this job?

_____

_____

_____

_____

What does a person with this job need to know to do their job well?

_____

_____

_____

LEARN MORE

Watch a video or read a book
about this occupation.

TITLE:_____

Notes:

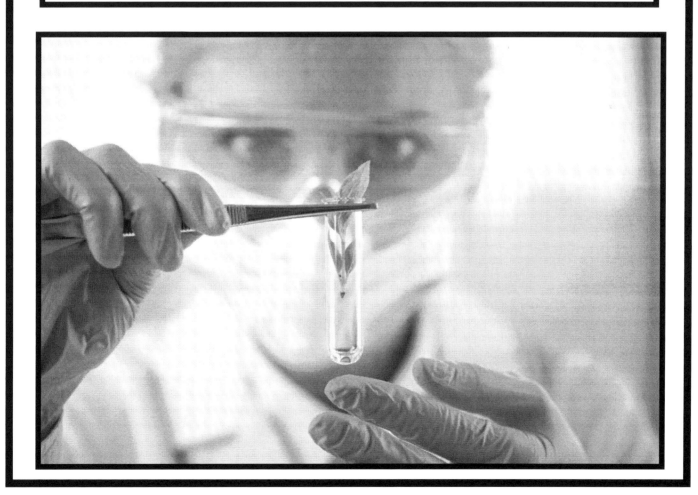

OCCUPATIONS
Would you like this job? YES - NO - MAYBE

Wetland Conservationist

What would the world be like if no one did this job?

_____

_____

_____

_____

_____

What does a person with this job need to know to do their job well?

_____

_____

_____

_____

LEARN MORE

Watch a video or read a book
about this occupation.

TITLE:_____

Notes:

OCCUPATIONS

Would you like this job? YES - NO - MAYBE

ENVIRONMENTAL SCIENTIST

What would the world be like if no one did this job?

_____

_____

_____

_____

_____

What does a person with this job need to know to do their job well?

_____

_____

_____

LEARN MORE

Watch a video or read a book
about this occupation.

TITLE:_____

Notes:

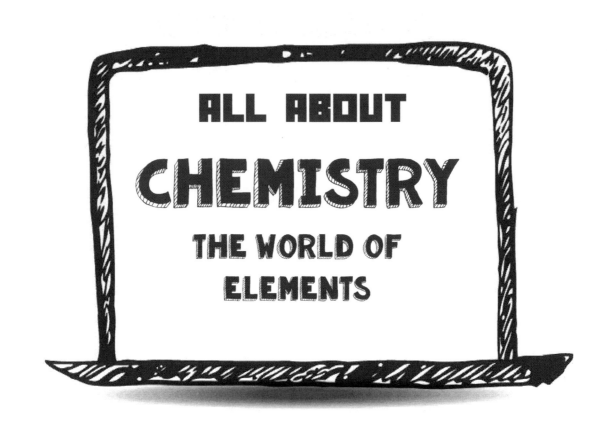

ALL ABOUT
CHEMISTRY
THE WORLD OF ELEMENTS

WHAT IS
CHEMISTRY?

Chemistry is a branch of physical science that studies the composition, properties, structure and change of matter.

Chemistry includes topics such as the properties of individual atoms, how atoms form chemical bonds to create chemical compounds, and the interactions of substances through intermolecular forces that give matter its general properties.

Chemistry also involves the interactions between substances through chemical reactions to form different substances.

MY BOOKS ABOUT
CHEMISTRY

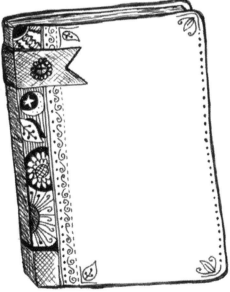
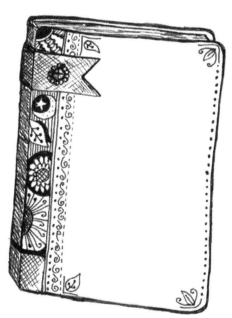

CHEMISTRY

READING TIME

Today's Date:

_____

Write and draw about what you are reading.

Date:

READING TIME
Copy an interesting or important paragraph or list from your book.
Book Title:_____ Page #_____

_____
_____
_____
_____
_____
_____
_____
_____
_____
_____
_____
_____
_____
_____
_____
_____
_____
_____

| Illustration 1 | Illustration 2 |

CHEMiSTry - THe WorLd oF ELeMeNtS

Try three different potion recipes in Minecraft.
Record your findings here.

My Notes

_____

_____

_____

_____

_____

_____

_____

_____

Brewing
in Minecraft 1.9

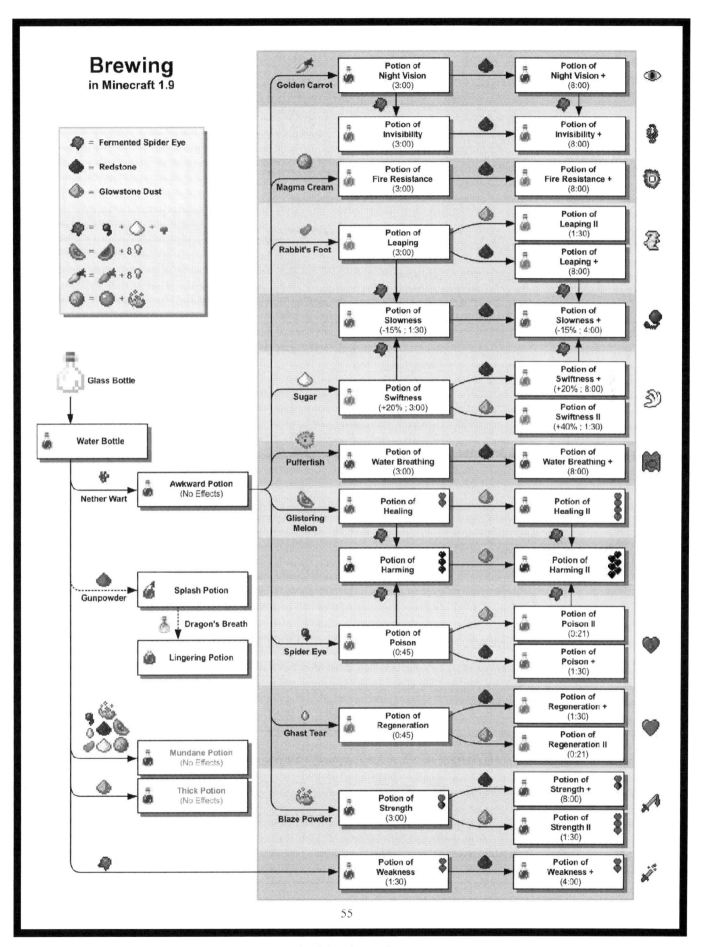

= Fermented Spider Eye

= Redstone

= Glowstone Dust

Glass Bottle

Water Bottle

Nether Wart

Awkward Potion
(No Effects)

Gunpowder

Splash Potion

Dragon's Breath

Lingering Potion

Mundane Potion
(No Effects)

Thick Potion
(No Effects)

Golden Carrot → Potion of Night Vision (3:00) → Potion of Night Vision + (8:00)

Potion of Invisibility (3:00) → Potion of Invisibility + (8:00)

Magma Cream → Potion of Fire Resistance (3:00) → Potion of Fire Resistance + (8:00)

Rabbit's Foot → Potion of Leaping (3:00) → Potion of Leaping II (1:30) / Potion of Leaping + (8:00)

Potion of Slowness (-15% ; 1:30) → Potion of Slowness + (-15% ; 4:00)

Sugar → Potion of Swiftness (+20% ; 3:00) → Potion of Swiftness + (+20% ; 8:00) / Potion of Swiftness II (+40% ; 1:30)

Pufferfish → Potion of Water Breathing (3:00) → Potion of Water Breathing + (8:00)

Glistering Melon → Potion of Healing → Potion of Healing II

Potion of Harming → Potion of Harming II

Spider Eye → Potion of Poison (0:45) → Potion of Poison II (0:21) / Potion of Poison + (1:30)

Ghast Tear → Potion of Regeneration (0:45) → Potion of Regeneration + (1:30) / Potion of Regeneration II (0:21)

Blaze Powder → Potion of Strength (3:00) → Potion of Strength + (8:00) / Potion of Strength II (1:30)

Potion of Weakness (1:30) → Potion of Weakness + (4:00)

55

Date:

WATCH A DOCUMENTARY ON CHEMISTRY

Title:_____

Draw a scene from the documentary:

Write a review:

_____
_____
_____
_____
_____

WHAT I LEARNED

Date:

Topic:_____

_____
_____
_____
_____
_____
_____
_____
_____
_____
_____
_____
_____
_____
_____
_____
_____

Draw a diagram or illustration:

Date:

_____

SCIENCE EXPERIMENTS & OBSERVATIONS

Look online, or in your science books, for an interesting chemistry experiment that you can do at home. Explain and draw the process and your findings here.

CREATE A MINECRAFT & SCIENCE
COMIC STRIP

Date:

CHEMISTRY
& THE
WORLD OF
ELEMENTS

VOCABULARY BUILDING

Look in your science books
for **FOUR** words with more than **TEN** letters.
Write the words and their definitions below:

MINECRAFT & THE REAL WORLD

What topic are you Learning About?

_____

Draw an example from Minecraft:

Draw an example from the real world:

MINECRAFT
DESIGN TIME

62

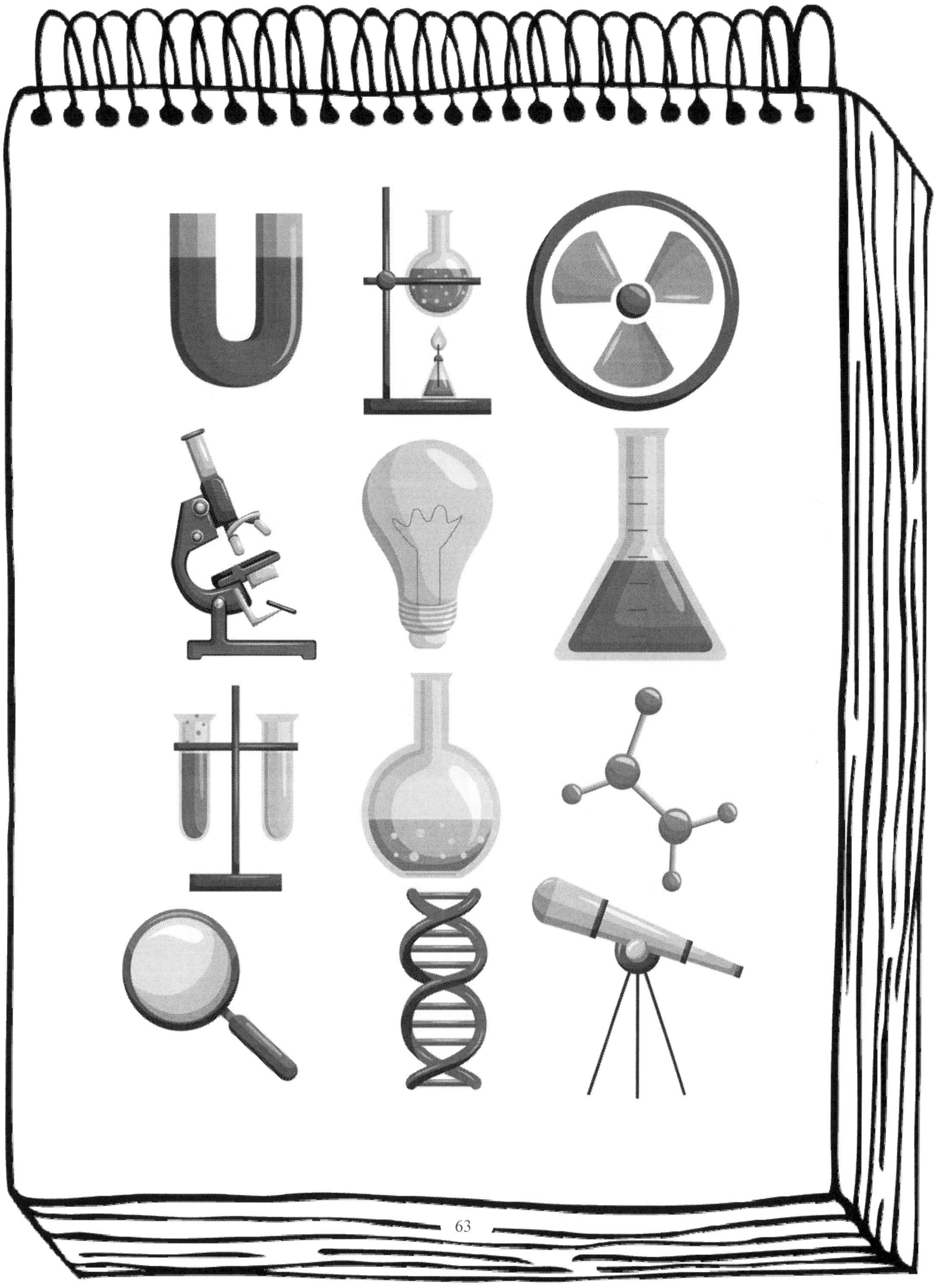

SCIENCE AND GEOGRAPHY

RESEARCH THE SCIENTIFIC DISCOVERY OF YOUR CHOICE:

WHERE IN THE
WORLD DID THE
DISCOVERY
TAKE PLACE?

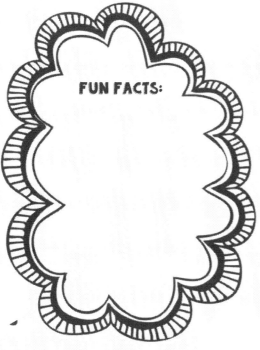

FUN FACTS:

DRAW THE DISCOVERY:

AMAZING SCIENTIFIC DISCOVERIES
CHOOSE A PERSON TO STUDY

Date:

Name:_____

BIOGRAPHY:

_____
_____
_____
_____
_____
_____
_____
_____
_____
_____
_____
_____
_____
_____
_____
_____

Draw a diagram or illustration:

CHEMISTRY LISTENING TIME
Draw and doodle
while listening to an audio book.

READING TIME

Today's Date:

_____

Write and draw about
what you are reading.

Date:

READING TIME

Copy an interesting or important
paragraph or list from your book.
Book Title:_____ **Page #**_____

_____
_____
_____
_____
_____
_____
_____
_____
_____
_____
_____
_____
_____
_____
_____
_____
_____

Illustration **1**

Illustration **2**

CHEMISTRY - THE WORLD OF ELEMENTS

Identify and list all the elements that exist in
Minecraft and in the real world.
Build a house using these items.

My List of Elements:

_____

_____

_____

_____

_____

_____

_____

_____

PERIODIC TABLE OF ELEMENTS

CHeMiSTry - THe WorLd oF ELeMeNTs

Periodic Table of MINECRAFT

Ore

C 16	**Fe** 15
Coal	Ferum
Au 14	**Ll** 21
Aurum	Lapis Lazuli
Rs 73	**Ad** 56
Redstone	Diamond

Natural

St 01	**Di** 03	**Sa** 12	**Be** 07	**Wd** 17	**Cl** 82
Stone	Dirt	Sand	Bedrock	Wood	Clay
Gr 13	**Sn** 80	**Ic** 79	**Gl** 20	**Cs** 04	**Mo** 48
Gravel	Snow	Ice	Glass	Cobblestone	Moss Stone
Ob 49	**Hm** 100	**MY** 110	**SP** 52	**Pk** 86	**Wl** 35
Obsidian	H.Mushroom	Mycelium	Spawner	Pumpkin	Wool

The Nether

Gs 89	**Fi** 51
Glowstone	Fire
Ne 87	**Nb** 112
Netherrock	NetherBrick
Ss 88	**NP** 90
Soul Sand	NetherPortal

Liquids

Aq 08	**Lv** 10
Aqua	Lava

The End

Es 121	**De** 122	**Ef** 122	**EP** 123
End Stone	Dragon Egg	E.P.Frame	End Portal

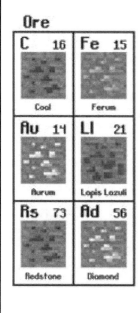
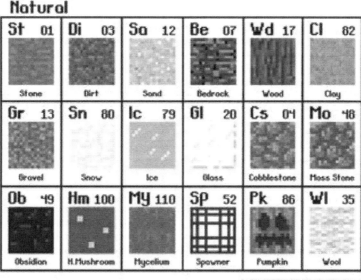
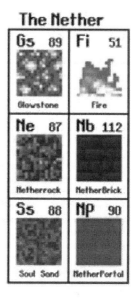

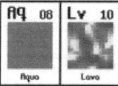

My Notes

_____
_____
_____
_____
_____
_____
_____
_____

Date:

WATCH A CHEMISTRY DOCUMENTARY

Title:_____

Draw a scene from the documentary:

Write a review:

_____
_____
_____
_____
_____

WHAT I LEARNED

Date:

Topic:_____

_____
_____
_____
_____
_____
_____
_____
_____
_____
_____
_____
_____
_____
_____
_____

Draw a diagram or illustration:

Date:

_____

SCIENCE EXPERIMENTS
& OBSERVATIONS

CREATE A MINECRAFT & SCIENCE
COMIC STRIP

Date:

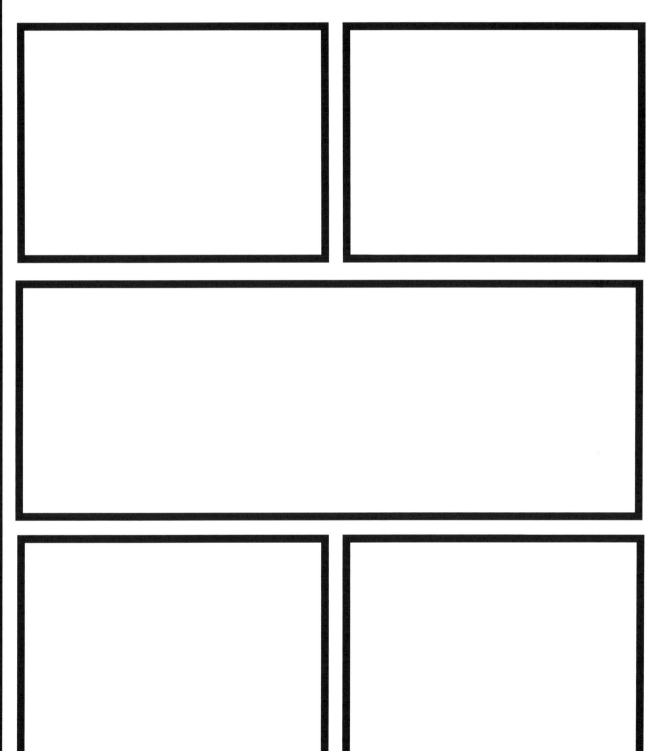

VOCABULARY BUILDING

Look in your science books
for **FOUR** words with more than **TEN** letters.
Write the words and their definitions below:

MINECRAFT & THE REAL WORLD

What topic are you Learning About?

_____

Draw an example from Minecraft:

Draw an example from the real world:

MINECRAFT
DESIGN TIME

SCIENCE AND GEOGRAPHY
RESEARCH THE SCIENTIFIC DISCOVERY OF YOUR CHOICE:

WHERE IN THE WORLD DID THE DISCOVERY TAKE PLACE?

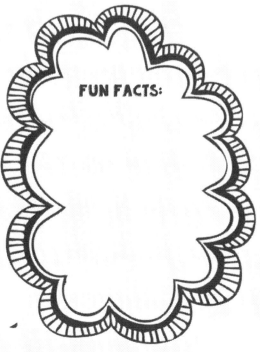

FUN FACTS:

DRAW THE DISCOVERY:

AMAZING SCIENTIFIC DISCOVERIES
CHOOSE A PERSON TO STUDY

Date:

Name: _____

BIOGRAPHY:

_____

_____

_____

_____

_____

_____

_____

_____

_____

_____

_____

_____

_____

_____

_____

Draw a diagram or illustration:

LISTENING TIME
Draw and doodle
while listening to an audio book.

OCCUPATIONS
Would you like this job? YES - NO - MAYBE

ANALYTICAL CHEMIST

What would the world be like if no one did this job?

_____

_____

_____

_____

_____

What does a person with this job need to know to do their job well?

_____

_____

_____

_____

LEARN MORE
Watch a video or read a book
about this occupation.

TITLE:_____

Notes:

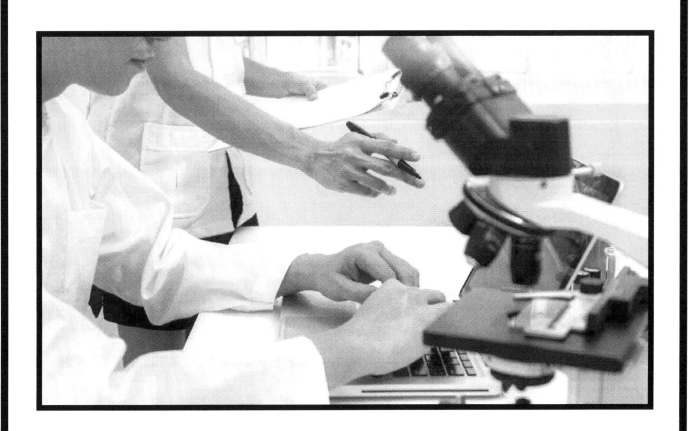

OCCUPATIONS

Would you like this job? YES - NO - MAYBE

CHEMICAL ENGINEER

What would the world be like if no one did this job?

_____

_____

_____

_____

_____

What does a person with this job need to know to do their job well?

_____

_____

_____

_____

LEARN MORE

Watch a video or read a book
about this occupation.

TITLE:_____

Notes:

OCCUPATIONS

Would you like this job? YES - NO - MAYBE

TOXICOLOGIST

What would the world be like if no one did this job?

_____

_____

_____

_____

_____

What does a person with this job need to know to do their job well?

_____

_____

_____

_____

LEARN MORE

Watch a video or read a book
about this occupation.

TITLE:_____

Notes:

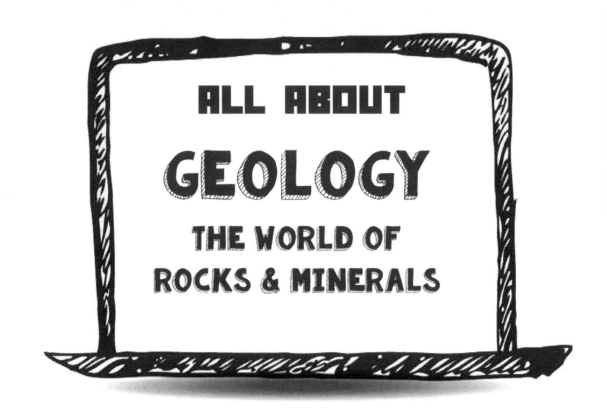

ALL ABOUT GEOLOGY
THE WORLD OF ROCKS & MINERALS

WHAT IS

GEOLOGY?

Geology is the science which deals with the physical structure and substance of the earth, their history, and the processes which act on them.

MY BOOKS ABOUT
GEOLOGY

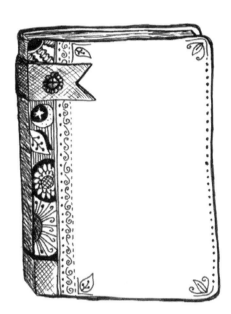
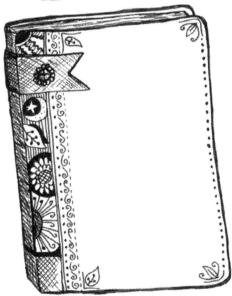
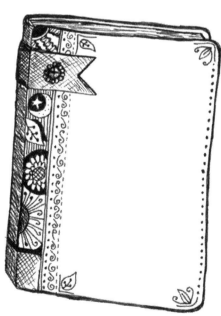

GEOLOGY

Today's Date:

_____

READING TIME

Write and draw about what you are reading.

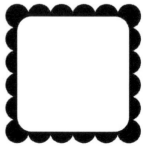

Date:

READING TIME
Copy an interesting or important paragraph or list from your book.
Book Title:_____ Page #_____

_____
_____
_____
_____
_____
_____
_____
_____
_____
_____
_____
_____
_____
_____
_____
_____
_____

Illustration 1

Illustration 2

Geology - The World of Rocks & Minerals

Look at the image on the right.
Design six layers of earth in your Minecraft World.

What elements did you use?

1.
2.
3.
4.
5.
6.

My Notes

Earth Layers Diagram

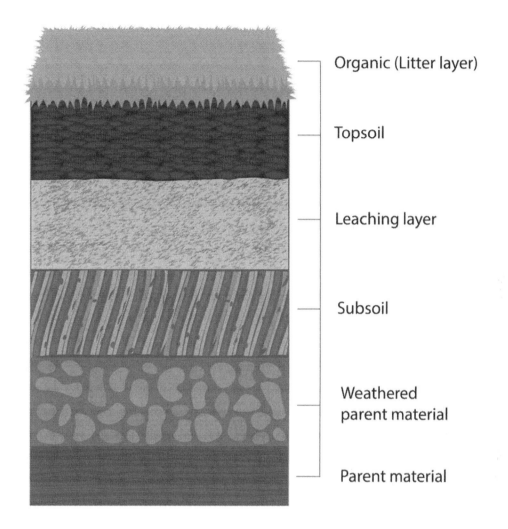

Organic (Litter layer)

Topsoil

Leaching layer

Subsoil

Weathered parent material

Parent material

My Notes

Date:

WATCH A GEOLOGY DOCUMENTARY

Title:_____

Draw a scene from the documentary:

Write a review:

_____
_____
_____
_____
_____

96

WHAT I LEARNED

Date:

Topic:_____

_____

_____

_____

_____

_____

_____

_____

_____

_____

_____

_____

_____

_____

Draw a diagram or illustration:

Date:

_____

SCIENCE EXPERIMENTS & OBSERVATIONS

CREATE A MINECRAFT & SCIENCE
COMIC STRIP

Date:

GEOLOGY
& THE
WORLD OF ROCKS
& MINERALS

VOCABULARY BUILDING

Look in your science books
for **FOUR** words with more than **TEN** letters.
Write the words and their definitions below:

MINECRAFT & THE REAL WORLD

What topic are you Learning About?

_____

Draw an example from Minecraft:

Draw an example from the real world:

MINECRAFT
DESIGN TIME

SCIENCE AND GEOGRAPHY

RESEARCH THE SCIENTIFIC DISCOVERY OF YOUR CHOICE:

WHERE IN THE WORLD DID THE DISCOVERY TAKE PLACE?

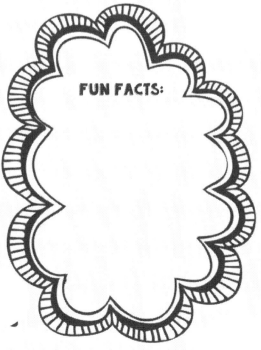

FUN FACTS:

DRAW THE DISCOVERY:

AMAZING SCIENTIFIC DISCOVERIES
CHOOSE A PERSON TO STUDY

Date:

Name: _____

BIOGRAPHY:

_____
_____
_____
_____
_____
_____
_____
_____
_____
_____
_____
_____
_____
_____
_____
_____

Draw a diagram or illustration:

GEOLOGY

LISTENING TIME
Draw and doodle
while listening to an audio book.

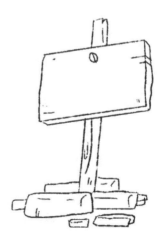

Today's Date:

READING TIME

Write and draw about what you are reading.

Date:

READING TIME
Copy an interesting or important paragraph or list from your book.
Book Title:_____ Page #_____

_____
_____
_____
_____
_____
_____
_____
_____
_____
_____
_____
_____
_____
_____
_____
_____

Illustration 1	Illustration 2

Geology - The World of Rocks and Minerals

Search your yard and neighborhood for rocks and minerals. Create a collection.
Draw and label all the rocks you find.

Geology - The World of Rocks and Minerals

Autochthonous sulfur in dolomites

Bornite with chalcopyrite

Galena

Chalcedony

Sphalerite

Variegated jasper

Auripigment

Amazonite

Flogopit

Lazurite

Rhodonite

Urite

Pyrope in eclogites

Serpentinite

Light blue calcite

Icelandic Spat

Plaster fragments

Bauxite solitov

Selenite plaster

Apatite grain

Magnesite

Fluorite Amazonian

Granite

Obsidian

Avanturin

Raspberry quartzite

Listvenite

Travertine

Pink marble

Ofiokalcit

My Notes

Date:

WATCH A DOCUMENTARY

Title:_____

Draw a scene from the documentary:

Write a review:

_____
_____
_____
_____
_____

WHAT I LEARNED

Date:

Topic: _____

_____
_____
_____
_____
_____
_____
_____
_____
_____
_____
_____
_____
_____
_____
_____

Draw a diagram or illustration:

Date:
_____

SCIENCE EXPERIMENTS & OBSERVATIONS

CREATE A MINECRAFT & SCIENCE
COMIC STRIP

Date:

VOCABULARY BUILDING

Look in your science books
for **FOUR** words with more than **TEN** letters.
Write the words and their definitions below:

MINECRAFT & THE REAL WORLD

What topic are you Learning About?

_____

Draw an example from Minecraft:

Draw an example from the real world:

MINECRAFT
DESIGN TIME

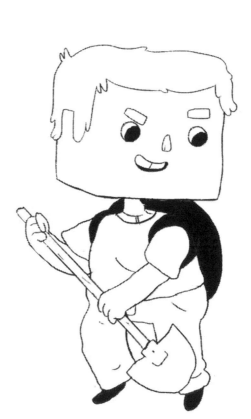

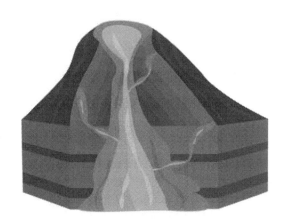
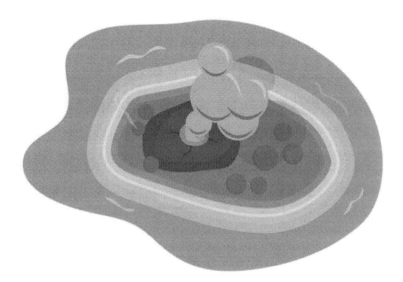

SCIENCE AND GEOGRAPHY

RESEARCH THE SCIENTIFIC DISCOVERY OF YOUR CHOICE:

WHERE IN THE WORLD DID THE DISCOVERY TAKE PLACE?

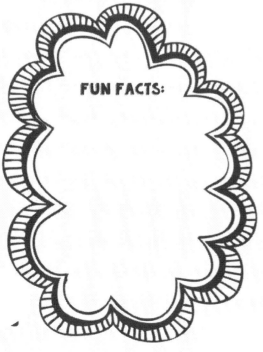

FUN FACTS:

DRAW THE DISCOVERY:

AMAZING SCIENTIFIC DISCOVERIES
CHOOSE A PERSON TO STUDY

Name: _____

BIOGRAPHY:

_____
_____
_____
_____
_____
_____
_____
_____
_____
_____
_____
_____
_____
_____
_____
_____
_____

Draw a diagram or illustration:

LISTENING TIME
Draw and doodle
while listening to an audio book.

Geology - The World of Rocks & Minerals
Let's Experiment!

What you will need:
1. A clear jar or bottle with a lid
2. Clean water
3. 4 or 5 different types of soil (sand, gravel, dirt, etc)

INSTRUCTIONS:

1. Fill your jar or bottle with water.
2. Put all the different types of soil into your jar.
3. Put the lid on and shake the jar/bottle until all the elements inside are well mixed.
4. Let the mixture sit for about 4 hours.

What happened to the mixture?
Write down your findings below.

My Notes

_____
_____
_____
_____
_____
_____
_____

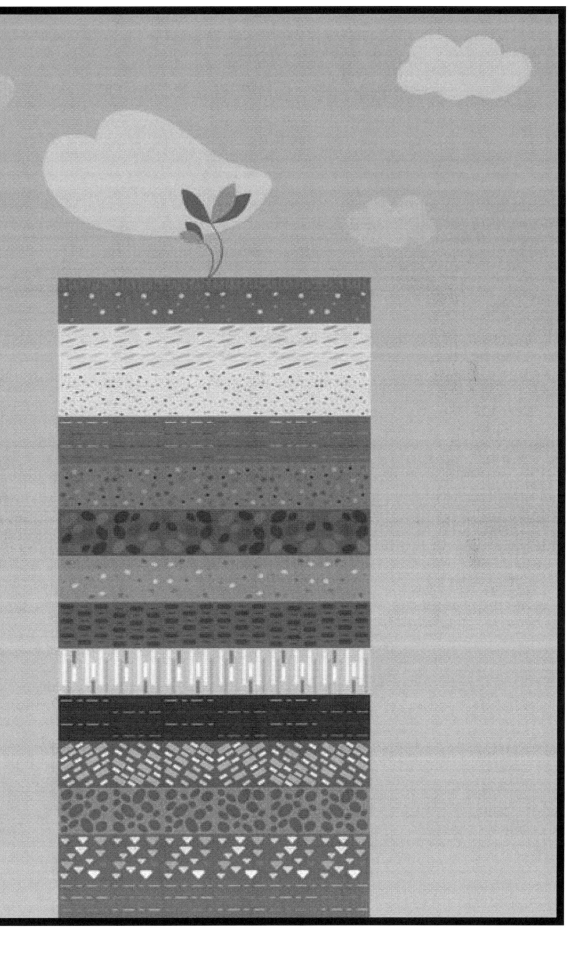

OCCUPATIONS

Would you like this job? YES - NO - MAYBE

GEOCHEMIST

What would the world be like if no one did this job?

_____
_____
_____
_____
_____

What does a person with this job need to know to do their job well?

_____
_____
_____
_____

LEARN MORE

Watch a video or read a book
about this occupation.

TITLE:_____

Notes:

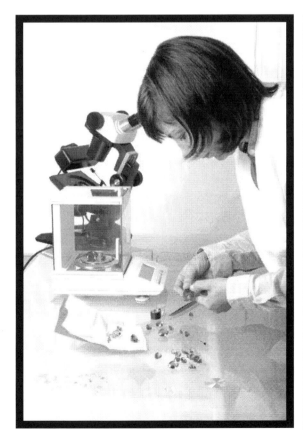

OCCUPATIONS

Would you like this job? YES - NO - MAYBE

GEOSCIENTIST

What would the world be like if no one did this job?

_____
_____
_____
_____
_____

What does a person with this job need to know to do their job well?

_____
_____
_____

LEARN MORE

Watch a video or read a book
about this occupation.

TITLE:_____

Notes:

OCCUPATIONS

Would you like this job? YES - NO - MAYBE

SEISMIC INTERPRETER

What would the world be like if no one did this job?

_____

_____

_____

_____

_____

What does a person with this job need to know to do their job well?

_____

_____

_____

_____

LEARN MORE

Watch a video or read a book
about this occupation.

TITLE:_____

Notes:

OCCUPATIONS

Would you like this job? YES - NO - MAYBE

ENGINEERING GEOLOGIST

What would the world be like if no one did this job?

_____

_____

_____

_____

_____

What does a person with this job need to know to do their job well?

_____

_____

_____

_____

LEARN MORE

Watch a video or read a book
about this occupation.

TITLE:_____

Notes:

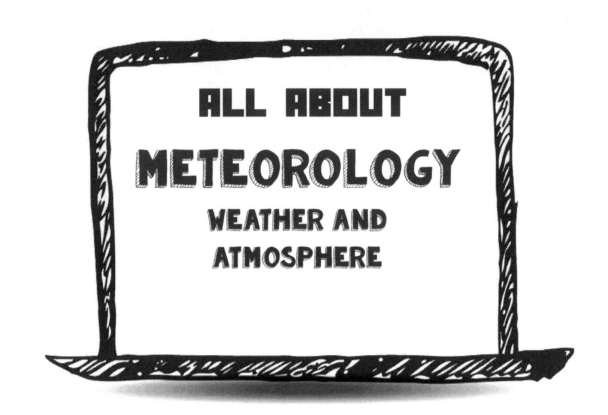

ALL ABOUT
METEOROLOGY
WEATHER AND ATMOSPHERE

WHAT IS
METEOROLOGY?

Meteorology is the scientific study of the atmosphere that focuses on weather processes and forecasting.

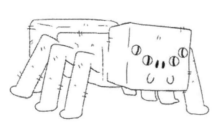

MY BOOKS ABOUT
METEOROLOGY

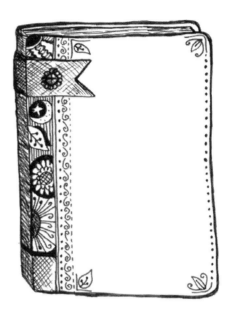
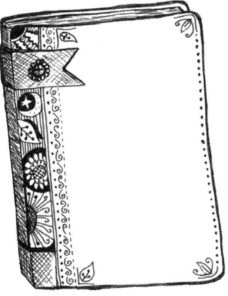
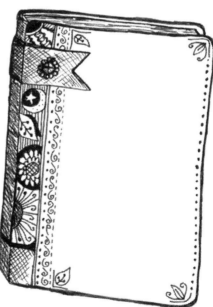

READING TIME

Today's Date:
_____

Write and draw about
what you are reading.

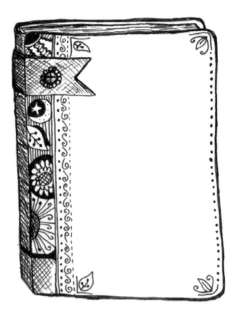

Date: _____

READING TIME

Copy an interesting or important
paragraph or list from your book.
Book Title:_____ Page #_____

_____
_____
_____
_____
_____
_____
_____
_____
_____
_____
_____
_____
_____
_____
_____
_____
_____
_____

Illustration 1	Illustration 2

Meteorology - Weather & Atmosphere

Look at the image on the right.

What kind of clouds are in Minecraft?
Go into your Minecraft world and find out!
Write down your answer below.

My Notes

_____
_____
_____
_____
_____
_____
_____
_____

CLOUDS

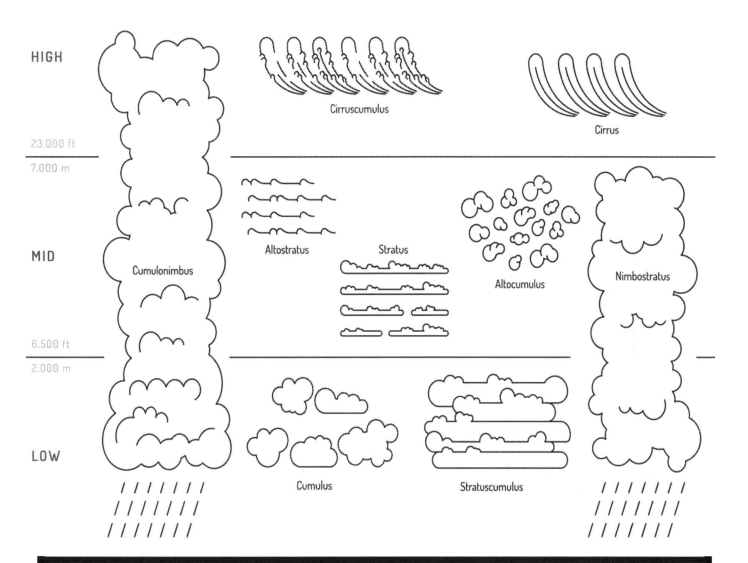

HIGH

23.000 ft
7.000 m

MID

6.500 ft
2.000 m

LOW

Cumulonimbus

Cirruscumulus

Cirrus

Altostratus

Stratus

Altocumulus

Nimbostratus

Cumulus

Stratuscumulus

My Notes

Date:

WATCH A DOCUMENTARY ON METEOROLOGY

Title:_____

Draw a scene from the documentary:

Write a review:
_____
_____
_____
_____
_____

WHAT I LEARNED

Topic:_____

_____

_____

_____

_____

_____

_____

_____

_____

_____

_____

_____

_____

_____

_____

_____

Draw a diagram or illustration:

Date:

SCIENCE EXPERIMENTS & OBSERVATIONS

CREATE A MINECRAFT & SCIENCE
COMIC STRIP

Date:

METEOROLOGY
WEATHER
AND
ATMOSPHERE

VOCABULARY BUILDING

Look in your science books
for **FOUR** words with more than **TEN** letters.
Write the words and their definitions below:

MINECRAFT & THE REAL WORLD

What topic are you Learning About?

_____

Draw an example from Minecraft:

Draw an example from the real world:

MINECRAFT
DESIGN TIME

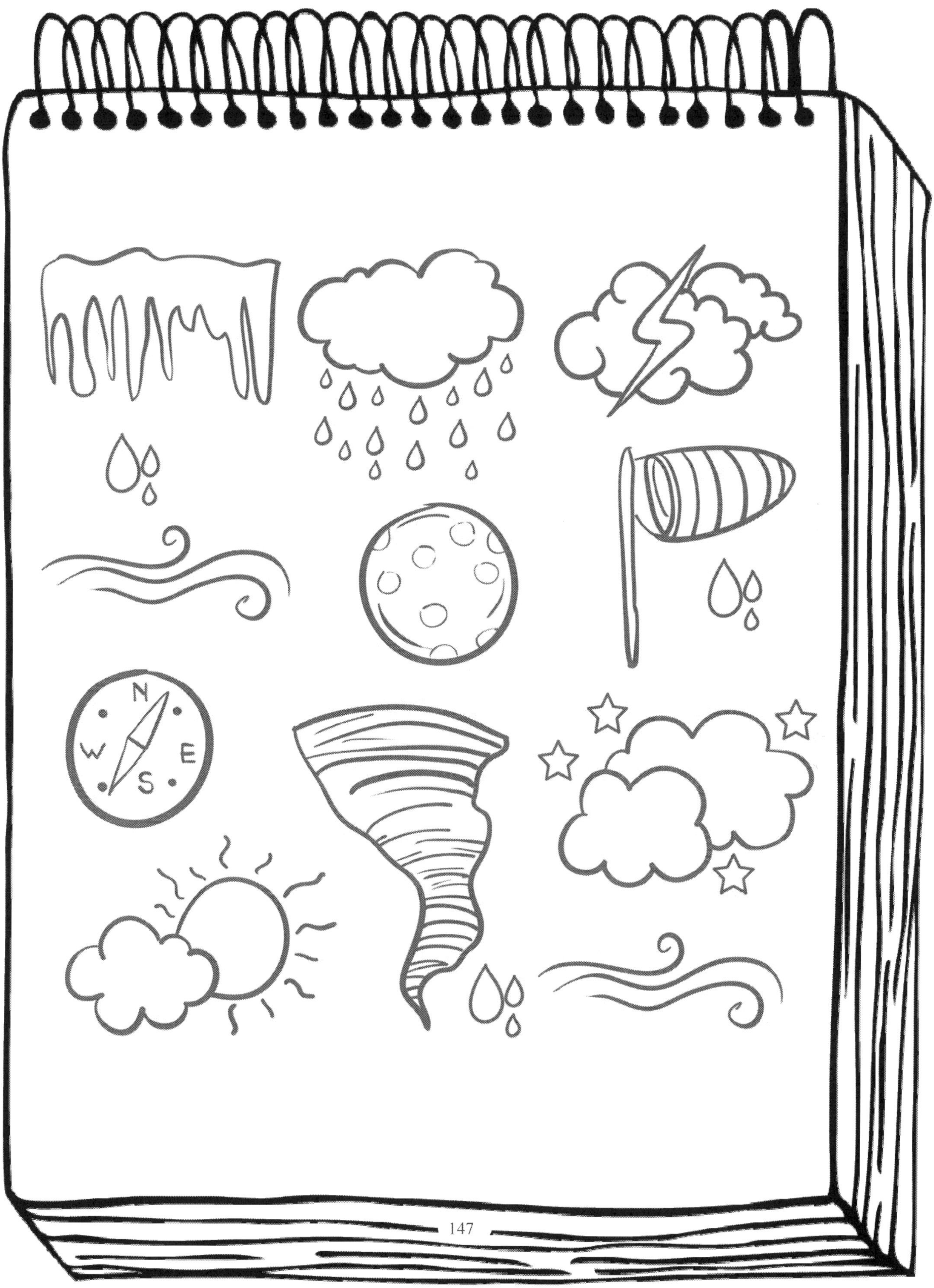
N
W
E
S

SCIENCE AND GEOGRAPHY

RESEARCH THE SCIENTIFIC DISCOVERY OF YOUR CHOICE:

WHERE IN THE WORLD DID THE DISCOVERY TAKE PLACE?

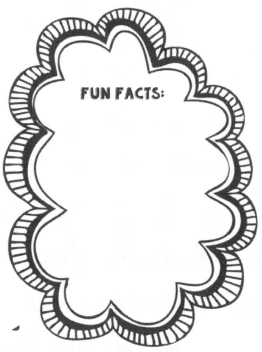

FUN FACTS:

DRAW THE DISCOVERY:

AMAZING SCIENTIFIC DISCOVERIES
CHOOSE A PERSON TO STUDY

Name:_____

BIOGRAPHY:

_____
_____
_____
_____
_____
_____
_____
_____
_____
_____
_____
_____
_____
_____
_____
_____
_____
_____

Draw a diagram or illustration:

LISTENING TIME
Draw and doodle
while listening to an audio book.

METEOROLOGY

Today's Date:

_____

READING TIME

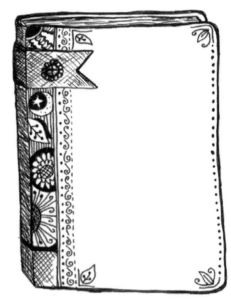

Write and draw about what you are reading.

Date:

READING TIME

Copy an interesting or important
paragraph or list from your book.
Book Title:_____ Page #_____

_____
_____
_____
_____
_____
_____
_____
_____
_____
_____
_____
_____
_____
_____
_____
_____
_____

Illustration 1

Illustration 2

Meteorology - Weather & Atmosphere

What's the weather?

1. Look at the weather forecast for the next three days.
2. Write down what the forecast says the next three days will be.
3. Watch, draw, and document what actually happens.

DRAW THE WEATHER TODAY:

Weather Forecast

DAY - 1

DAY - 2

DAY - 3

What actually happens

DAY - 1

DAY - 2

DAY - 3

Date:

WATCH A DOCUMENTARY

Title:_____

Draw a scene from the documentary:

Write a review:

_____
_____
_____
_____
_____

METEOROLOGY

WHAT I LEARNED

Date:

Topic:_____

_____
_____
_____
_____
_____
_____
_____
_____
_____
_____
_____
_____
_____
_____
_____
_____

Draw a diagram or illustration:

Date:

_____

SCIENCE EXPERIMENTS & OBSERVATIONS

_____
_____
_____
_____
_____
_____
_____
_____
_____
_____
_____
_____
_____

CREATE A MINECRAFT & SCIENCE
COMIC STRIP

Date:

159

VOCABULARY BUILDING

Look in your science books

for **FOUR** words with more than **TEN** letters.

Write the words and their definitions below:

MINECRAFT & THE REAL WORLD

What topic are you Learning About?

_____

Draw an example from Minecraft:

Draw an example from the real world:

MINECRAFT
DESIGN TIME

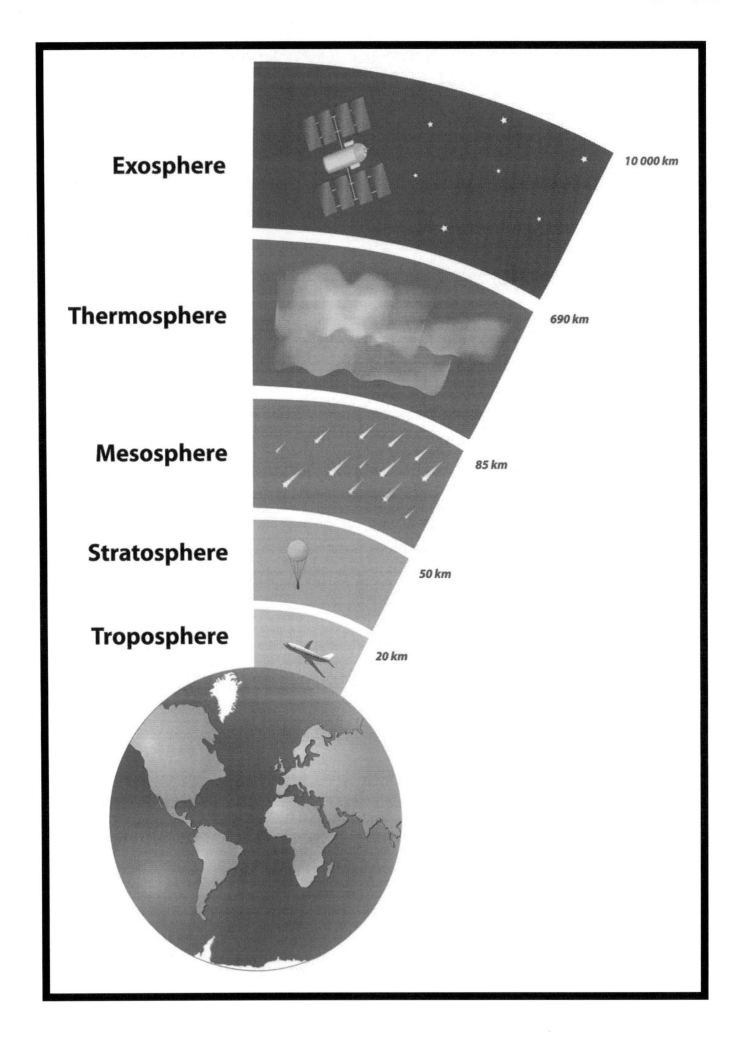

SCIENCE AND GEOGRAPHY

RESEARCH THE SCIENTIFIC DISCOVERY OF YOUR CHOICE:

WHERE IN THE WORLD DID THE DISCOVERY TAKE PLACE?

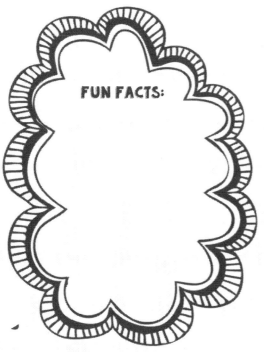

FUN FACTS:

DRAW THE DISCOVERY:

AMAZING SCIENTIFIC DISCOVERIES
CHOOSE A PERSON TO STUDY

Date:

Name: _____

BIOGRAPHY:

_____
_____
_____
_____
_____
_____
_____
_____
_____
_____
_____
_____
_____
_____
_____
_____
_____
_____

Draw a diagram or illustration:

METEOROLOGY

LISTENING TIME
Draw and doodle
while listening to an audio book.

OCCUPATIONS

Would you like this job? YES - NO - MAYBE

FORECASTER

What would the world be like if no one did this job?

_____

_____

_____

_____

_____

What does a person with this job need to know to do their job well?

_____

_____

_____

_____

LEARN MORE

Watch a video or read a book
about this occupation.

TITLE:_____

Notes:

OCCUPATIONS

Would you like this job? YES - NO - MAYBE

RESEARCH METEOROLOGIST

What would the world be like if no one did this job?

_____
_____
_____
_____

What does a person with this job need to know to do their job well?

_____
_____
_____

LEARN MORE
Watch a video or read a book
about this occupation.

TITLE:_____

Notes:

OCCUPATIONS
Would you like this job? YES - NO - MAYBE

MILITARY METEOROLOGIST

What would the world be like if no one did this job?

_____

_____

_____

_____

_____

What does a person with this job need to know to do their job well?

_____

_____

_____

_____

LEARN MORE

Watch a video or read a book
about this occupation.

TITLE:_____

Notes:

OCCUPATIONS
Would you like this job? YES - NO - MAYBE

TELEVISION METEOROLOGIST

What would the world be like if no one did this job?

_____

_____

_____

_____

_____

What does a person with this job need to know to do their job well?

_____

_____

_____

LEARN MORE

Watch a video or read a book
about this occupation.

TITLE:_____

Notes:

ALL ABOUT

PHYSICS

THE WORLD OF MATTER & ENERGY

WHAT IS

PHYSICS?

Physics is the branch of science concerned with the nature and the properties of matter and energy. The subject matter of physics includes mechanics, heat, light, radiation, sound, electricity, magnetism, and the structure of atoms.

MY BOOKS ABOUT
PHYSICS

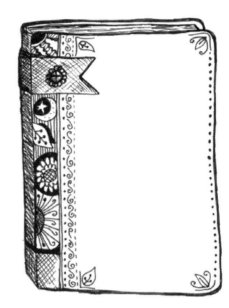

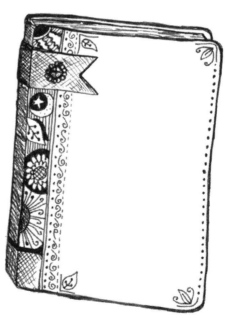

Today's Date:

_____

READING TIME

Write and draw about
what you are reading.

Date:

READING TIME
Copy an interesting or important paragraph or list from your book.
Book Title:_____ Page #_____

_____
_____
_____
_____
_____
_____
_____
_____
_____
_____
_____
_____
_____
_____
_____
_____
_____

Illustration 1

Illustration 2

Date:

WATCH A CHEMISTRY DOCUMENTARY

Title:_____

Draw a scene from the documentary:

Write a review:

_____
_____
_____
_____
_____

WHAT I LEARNED

Date:

Topic:_____

_____
_____
_____
_____
_____
_____
_____
_____
_____
_____
_____
_____
_____
_____
_____
_____

Draw a diagram or illustration:

Date:

_____

SCIENCE EXPERIMENTS & OBSERVATIONS

CREATE A MINECRAFT & SCIENCE
COMIC STRIP

Date:

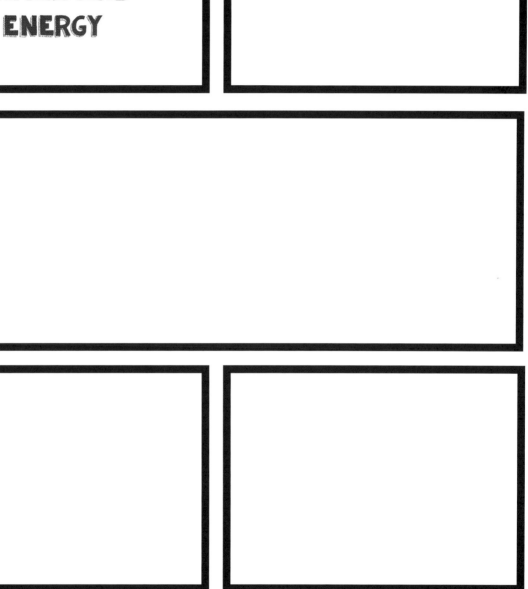

PHYSICS
THE WORLD OF
MATTER AND
ENERGY

VOCABULARY BUILDING

Look in your science books

for **FOUR** words with more than **TEN** letters.

Write the words and their definitions below:

MINECRAFT & THE REAL WORLD

What topic are you Learning About?

_____

Draw an example from Minecraft:

Draw an example from the real world:

MINECRAFT
DESIGN TIME

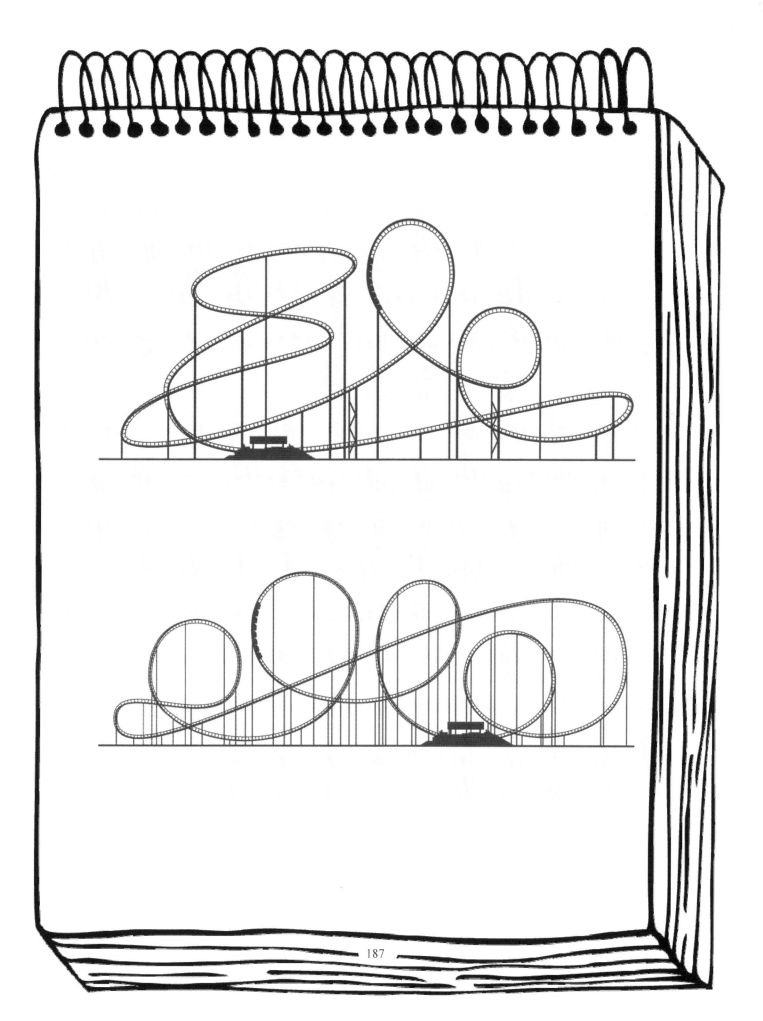

ART PAGE

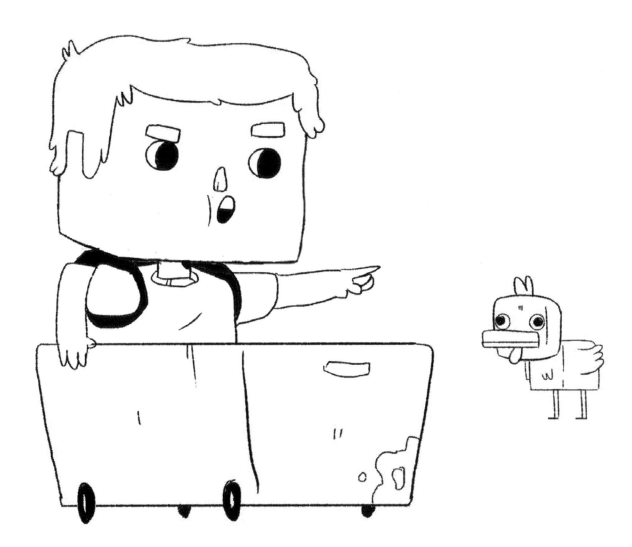

SCIENCE AND GEOGRAPHY
RESEARCH THE SCIENTIFIC DISCOVERY OF YOUR CHOICE:

WHERE IN THE WORLD DID THE DISCOVERY TAKE PLACE?

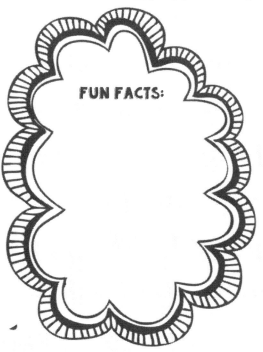

FUN FACTS:

DRAW THE DISCOVERY:

AMAZING SCIENTIFIC DISCOVERIES
CHOOSE A PERSON TO STUDY

Date:

Name: _____

BIOGRAPHY:

_____
_____
_____
_____
_____
_____
_____
_____
_____
_____
_____
_____
_____
_____
_____
_____

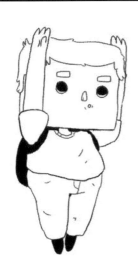

Draw a diagram or illustration:

LISTENING TIME
Draw and doodle
while listening to an audio book.

Today's Date:

_____

Write and draw about what you are reading.

Date:

READING TIME
Copy an interesting or important paragraph or list from your book.
Book Title:_____ Page #_____

_____

_____

_____

_____

_____

_____

_____

_____

_____

_____

_____

_____

_____

_____

_____

_____

Illustration 1	Illustration 2

Date:

WATCH A
DOCUMENTARY

Title:_____

Draw a scene from the documentary:

Write a review:

_____
_____
_____
_____
_____

PHYSICS

WHAT I LEARNED

Date:

Topic:_____

_____
_____
_____
_____
_____
_____
_____
_____
_____
_____
_____
_____
_____
_____
_____
_____
_____

Draw a diagram or illustration:

Date:
_____

SCIENCE EXPERIMENTS & OBSERVATIONS

CREATE A MINECRAFT & SCIENCE
COMIC STRIP

Date:

VOCABULARY BUILDING

Look in your science books

for **FOUR** words with more than **TEN** letters.

Write the words and their definitions below:

MINECRAFT & THE REAL WORLD

What topic are you Learning About?

_____

Draw an example from Minecraft:

Draw an example from the real world:

MINECRAFT
DESIGN TIME

SCIENCE AND GEOGRAPHY

RESEARCH THE SCIENTIFIC DISCOVERY OF YOUR CHOICE:

WHERE IN THE WORLD DID THE DISCOVERY TAKE PLACE?

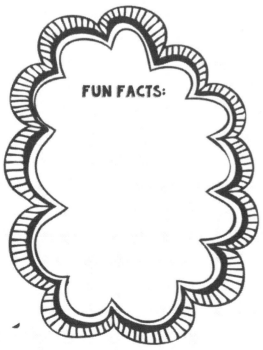

FUN FACTS:

DRAW THE DISCOVERY:

AMAZING SCIENTIFIC DISCOVERIES
CHOOSE A PERSON TO STUDY

Name:_____

BIOGRAPHY:

_____
_____
_____
_____
_____
_____
_____
_____
_____
_____
_____
_____
_____
_____
_____
_____
_____
_____

Draw a diagram or illustration:

PHYSICS

LISTENING TIME
Draw and doodle
while listening to an audio book.

OCCUPATIONS
Would you like this job? YES - NO - MAYBE

GEOPHYSICIST

What would the world be like if no one did this job?

_____

_____

_____

_____

_____

What does a person with this job need to know to do their job well?

_____

_____

_____

LEARN MORE

Watch a video or read a book
about this occupation.

TITLE: _____

Notes:

OCCUPATIONS

Would you like this job? YES - NO - MAYBE

METALLURGIST

What would the world be like if no one did this job?

_____

_____

_____

_____

What does a person with this job need to know to do their job well?

_____

_____

_____

LEARN MORE

Watch a video or read a book
about this occupation.

TITLE:_____

Notes:

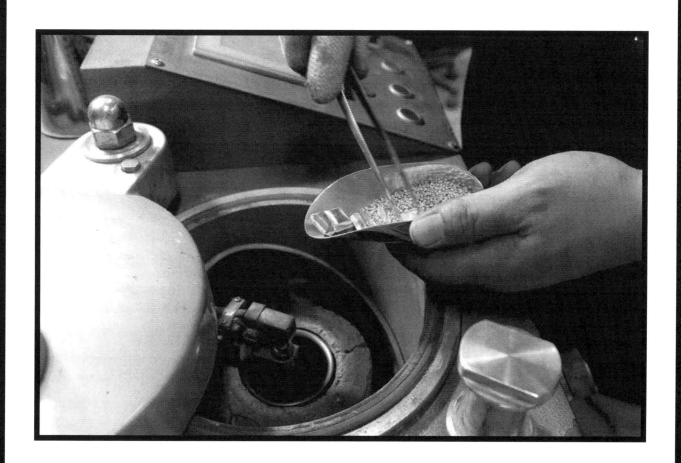

OCCUPATIONS

Would you like this job? YES - NO - MAYBE

NUCLEAR ENGINEER

What would the world be like if no one did this job?

_____
_____
_____
_____
_____

What does a person with this job need to know to do their job well?

_____
_____
_____
_____

LEARN MORE

Watch a video or read a book
about this occupation.

TITLE:_____

Notes:

ALL ABOUT

TECHNOLOGY

THE WORLD OF INVENTION AND DESIGN

WHAT IS

TECHNOLOGY?

Technology is
the branch of knowledge
that deals with the creation
and use of Technical
means and their
interrelation
with life, society, and the
environment.

212

MY BOOKS ABOUT
TECHNOLOGY

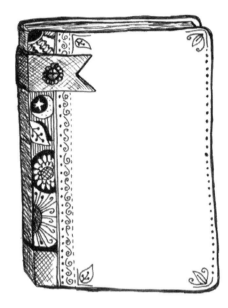
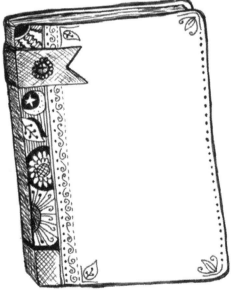
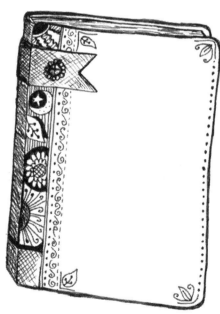

READING TIME

Today's Date:

_____

Write and draw about what you are reading.

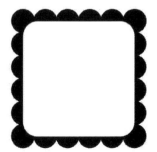

Date:

READING TIME

Copy an interesting or important paragraph or list from your book.

Book Title:_____ Page #_____

_____
_____
_____
_____
_____
_____
_____
_____
_____
_____
_____
_____
_____
_____
_____
_____
_____

Illustration 1	Illustration 2

Date:

WATCH A DOCUMENTARY ON TECHNOLOGY

Title:_____

Draw a scene from the documentary:

Write a review:
_____
_____
_____
_____
_____

216

WHAT I LEARNED

Date:

Topic:_____

_____
_____
_____
_____
_____
_____
_____
_____
_____
_____
_____
_____
_____
_____
_____
_____
_____

Draw a diagram or illustration:

Date:

_____

SCIENCE EXPERIMENTS & OBSERVATIONS

CREATE A MINECRAFT & SCIENCE
COMIC STRIP

Date:

TECHNOLOGY
THE WORLD OF INVENTION AND DESIGN

VOCABULARY BUILDING

Look in your science books
for **FOUR** words with more than **TEN** letters.
Write the words and their definitions below:

MINECRAFT & THE REAL WORLD

What topic are you Learning About?

_____

Draw an example from Minecraft:

Draw an example from the real world:

MINECRAFT
DESIGN TIME

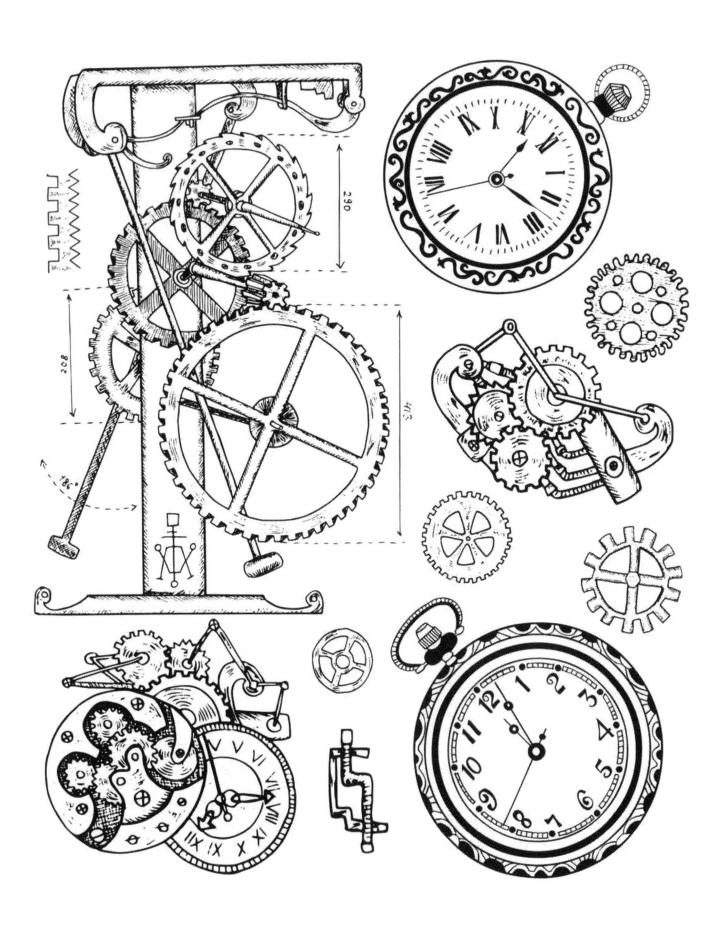

SCIENCE AND GEOGRAPHY
RESEARCH THE SCIENTIFIC DISCOVERY OF YOUR CHOICE:

WHERE IN THE
WORLD DID THE
DISCOVERY
TAKE PLACE?

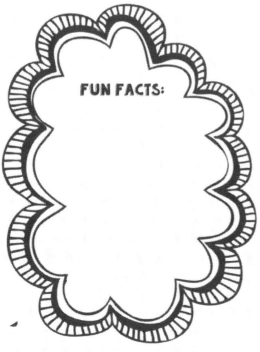

FUN FACTS:

DRAW THE DISCOVERY:

AMAZING SCIENTIFIC DISCOVERIES
CHOOSE A PERSON TO STUDY

Date:

Name: _____

BIOGRAPHY:

_____
_____
_____
_____
_____
_____
_____
_____
_____
_____
_____
_____
_____
_____
_____
_____
_____
_____

Draw a diagram or illustration:

TECHNOLOGY LISTENING TIME
Draw and doodle
while listening to an audio book.

Today's Date:

_____

READING TIME

Write and draw about what you are reading.

Date: _____

READING TIME
Copy an interesting or important
paragraph or list from your book.
Book Title:_____ **Page #**_____

_____
_____
_____
_____
_____
_____
_____
_____
_____
_____
_____
_____
_____
_____
_____
_____
_____
_____

Illustration 1	Illustration 2

Date:

WATCH A DOCUMENTARY

Title:_____

Draw a scene from the documentary:

Write a review:
_____
_____
_____
_____
_____

TECHNOLOGY WHAT I LEARNED

Topic: _____

_____

_____

_____

_____

_____

_____

_____

_____

_____

_____

_____

_____

_____

_____

_____

_____

_____

Draw a diagram or illustration:

Date:
_____

SCIENCE EXPERIMENTS & OBSERVATIONS

CREATE A MINECRAFT & SCIENCE
COMIC STRIP

Date:

VOCABULARY BUILDING

Look in your science books

for **FOUR** words with more than **TEN** letters.

Write the words and their definitions below:

MINECRAFT & THE REAL WORLD

What topic are you Learning About?

_____

Draw an example from Minecraft:

Draw an example from the real world:

MINECRAFT
DESIGN TIME

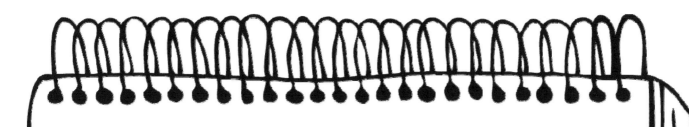

SCIENCE AND GEOGRAPHY

RESEARCH THE SCIENTIFIC DISCOVERY OF YOUR CHOICE:

WHERE IN THE WORLD DID THE DISCOVERY TAKE PLACE?

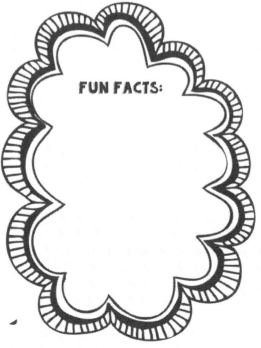

FUN FACTS:

DRAW THE DISCOVERY:

AMAZING SCIENTIFIC DISCOVERIES
CHOOSE A PERSON TO STUDY

Date:

Name: _____

BIOGRAPHY:

_____
_____
_____
_____
_____
_____
_____
_____
_____
_____
_____
_____
_____
_____
_____
_____

Draw a diagram or illustration:

TECHNOLOGY

LISTENING TIME
Draw and doodle
while listening to an audio book.

OCCUPATIONS

Would you like this job? YES - NO - MAYBE

PROGRAMMER

What would the world be like if no one did this job?

_____

_____

_____

_____

What does a person with this job need to know to do their job well?

_____

_____

_____

LEARN MORE

Watch a video or read a book
about this occupation.

TITLE:_____

Notes:

OCCUPATIONS

Would you like this job? YES - NO - MAYBE

WEB DEVELOPER

What would the world be like if no one did this job?

_____

_____

_____

_____

_____

What does a person with this job need to know to do their job well?

_____

_____

_____

_____

LEARN MORE

Watch a video or read a book
about this occupation.

TITLE:_____

Notes:

OCCUPATIONS
Would you like this job? YES - NO - MAYBE

SOFTWARE DEVELOPER

What would the world be like if no one did this job?

_____

_____

_____

_____

_____

What does a person with this job need to know to do their job well?

_____

_____

_____

_____

LEARN MORE
Watch a video or read a book
about this occupation.

TITLE:_____

Notes:

ALL ABOUT

ZOOLOGY

THE WORLD
OF ANIMALS

WHAT IS

ZOOLOGY?

Zoology is the study of animals and their behavior. Zoologists study animals and their interactions with ecosystems. They study their physical characteristics, diets, behaviors, and the impacts humans have on them.

MY BOOKS ABOUT
ZOOLOGY

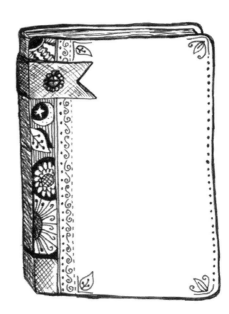

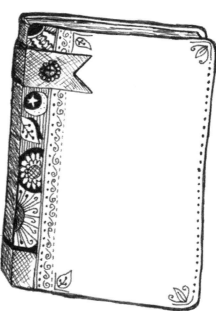

ZOOLOGY

Today's Date:
_____

READING TIME

Write and draw about what you are reading.

Date:

READING TIME
Copy an interesting or important
paragraph or list from your book.
Book Title:_____ **Page #**_____

_____
_____
_____
_____
_____
_____
_____
_____
_____
_____
_____
_____
_____
_____
_____
_____
_____
_____

Illustration 1	Illustration 2

Date:

WATCH A DOCUMENTARY ON ZOOLOGY

Title:_____

Draw a scene from the documentary:

Write a review:

_____
_____
_____
_____
_____

WHAT I LEARNED

Date:

Topic:_____

_____
_____
_____
_____
_____
_____
_____
_____
_____
_____
_____
_____
_____
_____
_____
_____
_____

Draw a diagram or illustration:

Date:

_____

SCIENCE EXPERIMENTS & OBSERVATIONS

CREATE A MINECRAFT & SCIENCE
COMIC STRIP

Date:

ZOOLOGY
AND THE WORLD
OF ANIMALS

VOCABULARY BUILDING

Look in your science books
for **FOUR** words with more than **TEN** letters.
Write the words and their definitions below:

MINECRAFT & THE REAL WORLD

What topic are you Learning About?

_____

Draw an example from Minecraft:

Draw an example from the real world:

MINECRAFT
DESIGN TIME

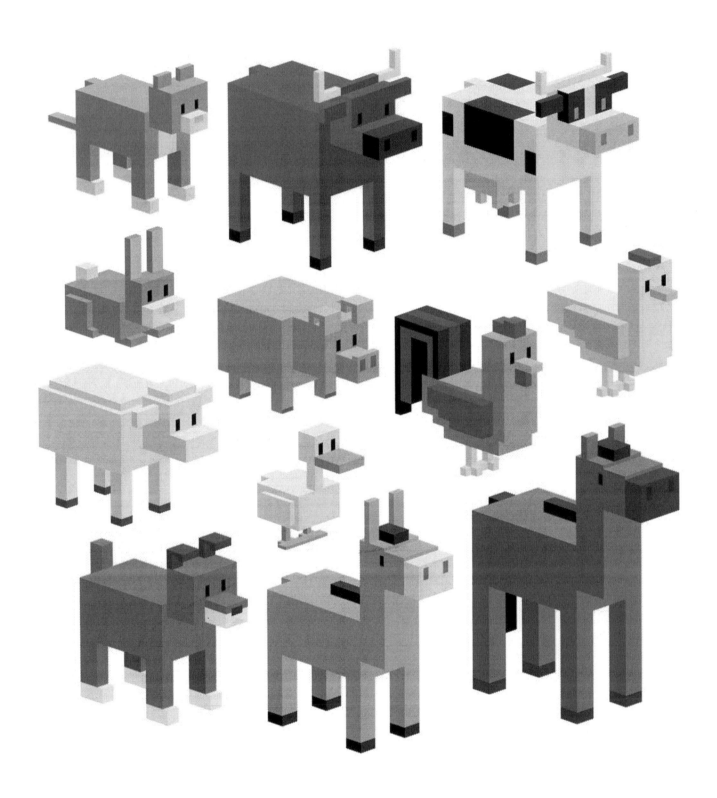

SCIENCE AND GEOGRAPHY

RESEARCH THE SCIENTIFIC DISCOVERY OF YOUR CHOICE:

WHERE IN THE WORLD DID THE DISCOVERY TAKE PLACE?

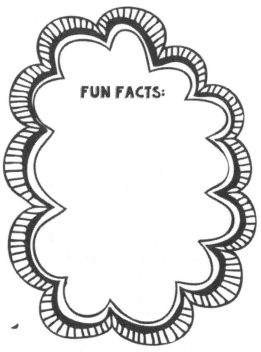

FUN FACTS:

DRAW THE DISCOVERY:

AMAZING SCIENTIFIC DISCOVERIES
CHOOSE A PERSON TO STUDY

Date:

Name: _____

BIOGRAPHY:

_____
_____
_____
_____
_____
_____
_____
_____
_____
_____
_____
_____
_____
_____
_____
_____
_____

Draw a diagram or illustration:

ZOOLOGY

LISTENING TIME
Draw and doodle
while listening to an audio book.

Today's Date:

READING TIME

Write and draw about what you are reading.

Date:

READING TIME
Copy an interesting or important paragraph or list from your book.
Book Title:_____ **Page #_____**

_____
_____
_____
_____
_____
_____
_____
_____
_____
_____
_____
_____
_____
_____
_____
_____
_____

Illustration 1

Illustration 2

Date:

WATCH A DOCUMENTARY

Title:_____

Draw a scene from the documentary:

Write a review:

_____
_____
_____
_____
_____

ZOOLOGY WHAT I LEARNED

Date:

Topic:_____

_____
_____
_____
_____
_____
_____
_____
_____
_____
_____
_____
_____
_____
_____
_____
_____

Draw a diagram or illustration:

Date:
_____

SCIENCE EXPERIMENTS & OBSERVATIONS

CREATE A MINECRAFT & SCIENCE
COMIC STRIP

Date:

VOCABULARY BUILDING

Look in your science books

for **FOUR** words with more than **TEN** letters.

Write the words and their definitions below:

MINECRAFT & THE REAL WORLD

What topic are you Learning About?

_____

Draw an example from Minecraft:

Draw an example from the real world:

MINECRAFT
DESIGN TIME

SCIENCE AND GEOGRAPHY

RESEARCH THE SCIENTIFIC DISCOVERY OF YOUR CHOICE:

WHERE IN THE WORLD DID THE DISCOVERY TAKE PLACE?

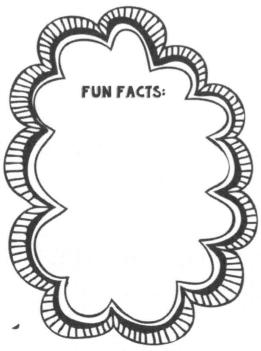

FUN FACTS:

DRAW THE DISCOVERY:

AMAZING SCIENTIFIC DISCOVERIES
CHOOSE A PERSON TO STUDY

Name:_____

BIOGRAPHY:

_____
_____
_____
_____
_____
_____
_____
_____
_____
_____
_____
_____
_____
_____
_____
_____
_____

Draw a diagram or illustration:

LISTENING TIME
Draw and doodle
while listening to an audio book.

OCCUPATIONS

Would you like this job? YES - NO - MAYBE

ZOO CURATOR

What would the world be like if no one did this job?

_____
_____
_____
_____
_____

What does a person with this job need to know to do their job well?

_____
_____
_____
_____

LEARN MORE

Watch a video or read a book
about this occupation.

TITLE:_____

Notes:

OCCUPATIONS

Would you like this job? YES - NO - MAYBE

WILDLIFE REHABILITATOR

What would the world be like if no one did this job?

_____

_____

_____

_____

_____

What does a person with this job need to know to do their job well?

_____

_____

_____

_____

LEARN MORE

Watch a video or read a book
about this occupation.

TITLE:_____

Notes:

OCCUPATIONS
Would you like this job? YES - NO - MAYBE

WILDLIFE BIOLOGIST

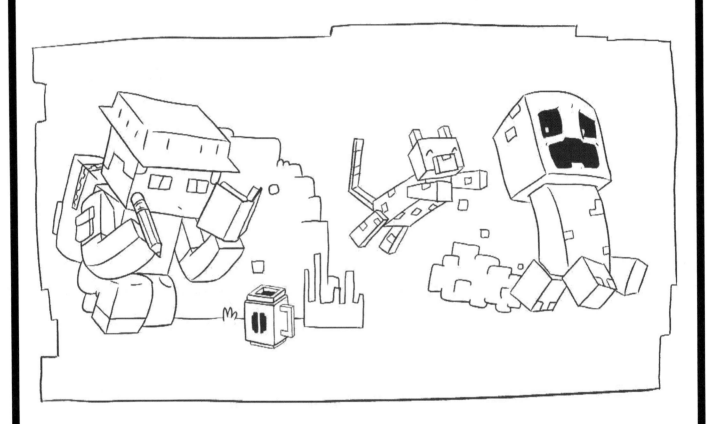

What would the world be like if no one did this job?

_____
_____
_____
_____
_____

What does a person with this job need to know to do their job well?

_____
_____
_____

LEARN MORE

Watch a video or read a book
about this occupation.

TITLE:_____

Notes:

OCCUPATIONS

Would you like this job? YES - NO - MAYBE

MARINE SCIENTIST

What would the world be like if no one did this job?

_____

_____

_____

_____

_____

What does a person with this job need to know to do their job well?

_____

_____

_____

_____

LEARN MORE

Watch a video or read a book
about this occupation.

TITLE:_____

Notes:

OCCUPATIONS

Would you like this job? YES - NO - MAYBE

WILDLIFE SANCTUARY DIRECTOR

What would the world be like if no one did this job?

_____

_____

_____

_____

_____

What does a person with this job need to know to do their job well?

_____

_____

_____

_____

LEARN MORE
Watch a video or read a book
about this occupation.

TITLE:_____

Notes:

DISCLAIMER:

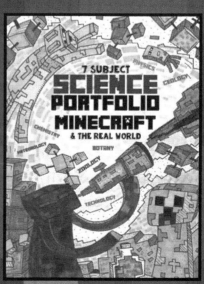